Confessions of a Reluctant Santa

THE LONG ROAD TO THE NORTH POLE

Joseph C. Leavitt

Reindeers Pause Publishing
Glendale, California

Cover and Interior Design by Peri Poloni,
Knockout Design, www.knockoutbooks.com

Cover Illustration by Amy Ritchie

Published in the United States of America by

Reindeers Pause Publishing
Glendale, California
www.reindeerspause.com

SAN: 256-2421
ISBN: 0-9762200-0-8

Dedication

This book is dedicated to
Andrea Steele-Leavitt,
my best friend and supporter—
and the best Mrs. Santa
in the world.

Special Thanks

A political figure not long ago suggested that it takes more than one person to raise a child. The same can be said of creating a book. And so, like a long-winded Academy Award speech, here is my list of special thanks.

Ericka Barber, Barbara Nielsen, and Teresa Nielsen-Hayden for their editing skills.

Gary Daines, Derick Fujimoto, Belma Johnson, and Miles and Bonnie Romney for their wonderful technical support.

Nello Manciatti, Peri Poloni and Amy Ritchie for their artistry.

Special thanks to the second and third grade classes of Sutter's Mill Elementary School taught by Mrs. Lishman and Mrs. Miller for writing from the heart.

Robert Cannaan, Dirk and Bonnie DeGraw, Mark and Denna Denton, Mario and Renee DiGregorio, David and Donna Jo Ellsworth, Debbie Gessel, Reena Hagerty, Reed Harrel, Jason and Jamie Meyers, Joe and Janice Paur, Jon and Judith Ritchie, Steve and Renee Stacy, Steven Steele, John Stothers, Sharon Tomlinson, and Marcus Van Doren for their support, input, and most of all, *friendship.*

Table of Contents

to SantaClause
from Joe

Dear Santa we love you just like
evry Body ells Dose You are
the best and just like my daddy
and you and my Familey are my
Favorite People in the whole World
we love you

We Love You

Chapter 1

The Mirror Doesn't Lie

(OR J.O.E. STANDS FOR JOLLY OLD ELF)

One of my fondest dreams for myself as I was growing up was to have matinee idol good looks accompanied by a well-toned muscular body. I never realized that dream. It was replaced by harsh reality, thanks to my gene pool and my propensity for sweets. Instead, I've become a significantly overweight middle-aged man more manatee than matinee. And, when I look in the mirror it is not a matinee idol that stares back, but rather a six-foot-six larger than life Father Christmas with a fluorescent white beard. I'm Joe Santa, not Joe Cool. I never wanted to be the Jolly Old Elf, but we all come to that inevitable moment in our lives when we must accept what is. Alas, the joke is on me. Ho, Ho, Ho!

People have been identifying me as Good St. Nick for some twenty years now. In fact, it doesn't matter where I go, what I'm wearing, or what time of year it is, children will point and say, "Look, Mommy, its Santa Claus!" Generally that statement is followed by the little tyke's putting his hands on his hips and demanding, "What are you doing here?" I suppose they think Santa should spend all his free time at the North Pole, making toys. I was very annoyed when that first began to happen and would usually retort with, "Isn't there a freeway you can go play on, kid?" Now I just hand the apologetic parents a card with a picture of me as Santa Claus, and tell them my rate for a personal visit. I had to get over being offended by being called "Santa" a long time ago.

There is also the occasional little moppet who mistakes me for Jesus. First of all, I doubt Christ ever needed Weight Watchers, and, secondly, what did you smoke for lunch, kid? As an actor I have been cast in biblical roles, but the closest I ever got to portray the Son of God was playing Peter, who was written as an over-sized wine bibbing sot, in a musical effluent called "Magdalene". Usually I'm cast as the antithesis of Jesus. Among the New Testament villains I have played are Herod, who beheaded John the Baptist, (Crystal Cathedral's Easter pageant), and Caiaphas, the high priest who condemned Christ to death in a film called "The Testaments".

Once while I was visiting California Adventure at Disneyland, a kid tapped me on the leg and chirped, "Hi, Big Bird!" Big Bird? Santa Claus, yes. May-be Jesus, if you really, really stretch it. But, Big Bird? I have never had feathers, webbed feet, or a big orange beak, and neither was I wearing yellow. Big Bird, indeed!

Dear Santau,

Is it troo that you are magcle?

Santau without you I wold be misruble, thankyou

Love, Liam

Chapter 2

How Did I Ever Get to Where I Am, When I Never Wanted to be Here in the First Place

(OR DE-NILE ISN'T JUST A RIVER IN ENGLAND)

As I mentioned in the last chapter, I never wanted to be Santa Claus. So, how did I end up transforming? For years I was barraged by people telling me I'd make a perfect Santa Claus. But we seldom see ourselves as others do. The observation annoyed me because I didn't want anyone else defining who I was or what kinds of roles I should play. I was in a rather profound state of denial. While I was desperately trying to see myself as sexy and swashbuckling, choreographers, casting directors, and pretty much everyone else saw me as a gigantic bearded Pillsbury Dough Boy.

Early in my acting career, I was up for a Japanese commercial, where they were looking for a pirate. The casting session was bizarre. There were at least ten people in front of the room all speaking very animatedly to each other in Japanese. One of them stepped forward and said, "Please take off shirt." I complied. My action caused another outbreak of animated Japanese. It ended with the interpreter stepping forward again and saying, "Please put shirt back on! They say you would make good Santa." It was as if God stretched out His hand at that point and decreed, "You're Santa Claus. Deal with it!"

Size wasn't the only thing. Not only was I in denial about my look, I also refused to admit that stage dance (or movement as we call it in the biz) was not exactly my forte. Everyone used to tell me I was light on my feet. Everyone was wrong. In reality, when it came to dance ability; I ran the complete gamut from pathetic to absolutely hopeless. Most choreographers saw me as a minion of the anti-Christ, and would force me into the back during production numbers. Debbie Reynolds was not exactly enamored of my inability to trip the light fantastic either. When we attempted to prepare a number for a Lana Turner roast, looking dubiously at me, she sighed, "Shades of Eddie Fisher; he couldn't dance either!"

On another occasion, I was in a ball room scene for a commercial with my friend Marilyn Hickey-Rehring. The shoot lasted most of the day and we had to spend the entire time waltzing. (The things you'll put yourself through for a hundred and fifty bucks!) All the while I kept stepping on her feet and bumping her with my right knee. It was a ballroom disaster. I'm surprised she can still walk upright and even more that she still speaks to me.

Poor Carol Swarbrick, whom I consider one of the great musical theater actresses of our time, played opposite me in "The New Moon", and she fared little better. She tried to make sure I didn't look like a total prat when our scenes called for bits and pieces of choreography. I'm sure I sent her to her dressing room sobbing more than once. If it hadn't been for her infinite patience with me, which alone will secure her a place in Heaven, I would have sunk like the Titanic.

When I played Buffalo Bill in "Annie Get Your Gun", the choreographer threatened to have me killed. So, I worked and worked and worked until I achieved a state of not completely awful. It was a lot like trying to teach synchronized swimming to a beached whale. The critics, when reviewing me, went with a more "Buffalo than Bill" theme; one called me grotesque, another said I pranced through the role, while yet another claimed I lumbered through the entire show.

Ouch! All the while a little voice kept saying, "Don't you think it's time you put away your dance shoes and embrace your inner Santa Claus?"

But I resisted. Still not wanting to yell, "Uncle", about my two left feet, I began taking classes. The first was ballet. I hated bellying up to the barre as it were because it was next to the mirror. I was aghast as I could see what looked rather like a walrus in a tutu attempting plies and pirouettes. I never tried any grand jetes (leaps) for fear they would register on the Richter scale. Though the ballet mistress did say I had pretty good balance, I lasted only one session. My jazz and tap classes were equally short-lived and both ended in great weeping, wailing, and gnashing of teeth; not mine of course, but the instructor's and the class members' whom I had injured by running into or stepping upon.

In an epiphany of reality, I finally had to stop beating a dead horse; my brain was never going to connect with my feet. I also had to throw in the towel on ever playing a leading man unless it was in "Miracle on 34th Street". So to paraphrase, Robert Frost, "Two roads diverged in a yellow wood, and sorry I could not travel both, I took the one that led to the North Pole."

Dear Santa
How fare is the
north Pol?
I love your
Presints.
wen is your
birthDay?
I can't wait
tell chrismis.
Love Kycie

Dear Santa,
I wood licke for christmas
a Bratdoll. Santa thank you
for the thing you do.
Do you reely have Elfs.
We will giv you cocys
and milk and carits.
What are your radys names.

Thank you

Love Ellie

Chapter 3

I'm Ready for my Santa Close Up, Mr. DeMille

(OR BY GEORGE, I THINK HE'S GOT IT!)

Despite my adult aversion to Mr. Claus, as a kid I always liked Santa, or at least the idea of him. Think about it. Here's a jolly old guy in a red suit flying across the sky to deliver toys to me, plain old Joe. Toys that I didn't even have to earn. How great was that?

My first recollection of St. Nick is as a four-year-old. I was at a church Christmas dinner with my family and toward the end of dessert; I heard sleigh bells from outside. Moments later, Santa appeared. I was spellbound. I don't remember sitting on his lap, but I do remember his giving me a small bag of hard candy. I didn't have the candy long because my older sister grabbed it from me and proceeded to devour it. She was always pulling stuff like that when we were kids. Her philosophy was, "What's mine is mine, and what's yours is mine." It was almost like living with the I.R.S.

.I was seven when I had my next personal encounter with Papa Noel. My father gave me a dollar to go Christmas shopping, so I trekked from our house to Main Street in a very few minutes. Upon entering the J.J. Newberry store, I spotted Santa. I quickly got in line with absolutely no forethought of what I might ask for. When I reached his lap my mind was a blank. I could think of nothing to ask for but a football. A football? Even then, I was painfully aware of my inadequacies when it came to sports; especially football. (I did go out for football in high school. Not for the love of the game, only to impress the girls so I could get dates. I was cut after a week so I never played in a game, and, the closest thing I ever had to a date was a cheerleader telling me she had to do her nails and couldn't possibly go out with me. It's particularly gratifying to go to high school reunions now and see how heavy-handed Mother Nature has been with the cheerleaders. Even as an actor, football never served me well. I was cast in the Coke commercial for 1998 Super Bowl. I had visions of it playing for a long time, and getting me out of debt. Dollar signs were dancing in my head. Alas, it yielded few dollars. It ended up being the lowest rated ad in Super Bowl history, and only aired that day.) I point this out only to underline the absurdity of my asking for a football from Santa.

I had no more personal interaction with Jolly Old St. Nicholas till I was twenty-four. A friend asked me to act as the Seasonal Elf for her church Christmas party. I'm sure the consideration was, "Let's get the biggest, fattest guy we know to play Santa Claus. I know, we'll ask Joe!" This time I wasn't sitting on his lap. This time, I had to put on the suit and somehow assume the persona of Santa! Harboring great reservations about doing it, I nearly had an anxiety attack waiting for my entrance. You'd think being an actor I could have handled the situation, but it ended abysmally. When I came running in with my overly enthusiastic "Ho! Ho! Ho!" the fake beard flew off and the pants fell immediately to my ankles. The audience responded with raucous laughter while I fervently prayed for the angel of death to come and take me right then and there.

Nearly ten years elapsed before I picked up the Red Suit again. I was paid fifty bucks by a group of merchants in a small shopping district to mingle amongst yuletide revelers on the street. I fared little better than my first foray into Jolly Old Elfdom. The costume was ill fitting and the pants fell to the ground after a few minutes. (It was years before I finally came to the conclusion that just may-be suspenders would help to keep my Santa trousers up!) Subsequently the beard began to sag and a group of pre-pubescent children pointed and began yelling, "You're a fake! You're a fake!" I was rather gratified when their mother gave them a smack and demanded that they stop spoiling the illusion. To make matters worse the merchants had hired a second rate accordion player to accompany my act and he made all of the Christmas carols sound like "Lady of Spain." I vowed that evening to never ever play Santa again.

But a funny thing happened before the end of the gig, which seemed longer than my first marriage, a three-year-old boy tugged on my leg. I hunched down to talk with him. Genuinely excited to see me, his eyes sparkled as he told me what he wanted for Christmas. He then gave me a great big hug. And, I thought, "May-be this isn't so bad."

Dear santa thank you
for all of the stuff
you DO for us we
love chrismas It
fun to visit with
falimy frinds
what Dose chrismis
land on this year
I Love evurything
that you give to
me I play with
no mater what
there rilly spicsel
to me. thank you
for evrything I cant
wait till this chrismis.
I happy Its coming
up
                    LOVE Mackenzie

Dear Santa,
Today is my B day!!!
        Merry Christmas!

                Trini

ps. Are you Christian

        I am

Chapter 4

Putting Away Childish Things

(OR REALITY BITES)

The process of growing up and becoming an adult is often painful and requires the periodic putting away of childish things. I suppose one of those things is a belief in mythical heroes. I have often wondered how many people stretched out on a therapist's couch have been able to trace their problems back to the trauma they experienced when their bubble was burst about Santa Claus.

I began to question the verity of the Jolly Christmas Visitor when I was six. That Christmas, my sisters and I received a nicely made child size table with matching benches. When my mother made a big deal about how our friend had crafted the miniature dinette, my stomach was in knots. Surely if there were a present under the tree, the Man in Red had to have made it, didn't he? If indeed this present hadn't been crafted in the North Pole, then that could mean the rest of the presents...I wouldn't let myself finish the thought. My whole childish belief system was on the brink of collapse. Surely adults wouldn't have been lying to me all this time. My confidence in Santa began to crumble, but I desperately held onto my belief in him till the next Christmas. My older sister, the one who systematically relieved me of my candy and money, took great pleasure in taking Santa Claus away from me as well. It's funny. I was rather calm about the news. I was more upset at eighteen when I found out Betty Crocker wasn't real! This makes sense when you realize I have a very close personal relationship with food!

There is a sense of loss when a "childish thing" is put away. Almost out of necessity, it needs to be replaced with something else. I replaced my childish belief in Santa with the accordion. When I announced to my mother at age eight I wanted to learn to play the accordion, she toyed with the idea of selling me to the gypsies, and then with a sigh acquiesced to my desire. I have played the accordion in several different venues throughout my acting career even in the aforementioned Super Bowl Coke commercial. Once, in a staged production of Charles Dickens' "A Christmas Carol," portraying the Ghost of Christmas Present, I had to play the concertina whilst I strode about the stage atop eighteen-inch railroad ties. Don't ask! But, I've never used the squeezebox as part of my Santa work. I think the Red Suit is scary enough to most kids. Add an accordion; well, you do the math.

Dear santa

My name is Foster. I have been a very good boy.
I got A's on my math and spelling tests. I am in first grade. For Christmas, I would like Batman and the Jokers and wrestlers, spiderman and power rangers.
Thank you Santa.

Love Foster

Chapter 5

Fodder for the Therapist

(OR WHAT DO YOU MEAN, I SOUND JUST LIKE MY FATHER?!)

I am not really sure why I had such an adversarial relationship with my father growing up. It may have something to do with his making me learn to work. I hated work. It cut into my favorite activity, sitting and doing nothing. I felt it was my divine right to go through life just having a good time. Leave work to those not smart enough to get out of it. In my formative years, I was quite sure my paternal progenitor had a limited understanding of how the world functions. While I, young as I was, was sure I had all of the answers.

In fact, considering myself a prodigy, I thought I was smarter than my entire family. I only tolerated them because I had no other choice. Being seen with them was a never-ending source of embarrassment and emotional pain. I had no desire to be related to them in any way, especially, my dad. It's interesting in light of my juvenile mind set, that I spent so much time in my early life attempting to gain his approval.

My modus operandi growing up was to make sure I was as different from my father as possible. His folksiness and corny jokes irritated me. I would never ever be like him, not in a million years. We would always be separate entities with nothing in common. There were times on Christmas Eve when Dad would dress as Santa Claus and visit my cousins. I thought he looked absolutely ridiculous and vowed I would never dress up in a stupid Santa suit, just to perpetuate an idiotic Myth for gullible children. No, I would never be that ridiculous. Me, wear a Santa suit? Not for all the tea in China!

But Mother Nature has a way of putting us in our place. Don't you just hate that? With the passage of time she has shown me that, in fact, I was not a prodigy, and that my dad was a heck of a lot smarter than I realized. I find myself at this juncture in life shrinking back in horror and asking, "When did I become my father?" I also find myself being just as corny and folksy as Dad was. Worst of all, I even inherited his ridiculous desire to dress as Santa, and not just on Christmas Eve. I have managed to parlay playing Santa into a career. I suppose a good psychotherapist could explain to me just how and when it was that I became my father; but I'm not sure my Santa insurance would cover it.

Dear Santa,

I have been a good girl.

Here is my list if you please.
- Video now spongebob
- operation
- Barbie's
- Anything else

I love you and I hope you like the mile and cookies.

The carrots are for Rudolf

Madeleine

Chapter 6

Eat, Drink, and be Merry for Tomorrow Ye Diet

(OR YOU'RE NOT FAT, YOU'RE JUST A BIG GUY)

One of my greatest passions is food. In Isaiah 55 we read, "...eat ye that which is good, and let your soul delight in fatness." A good Santa will take that advice to heart. I certainly have. I love to eat. I shall be distraught if in the next life I get there and find no chocolate, watermelon, coconut cream pie, prime rib, or Rice Krispy treats. Loving food as much as I do has made it virtually impossible to control my weight. The first word most children utter is either "mama" or "dada." My first word came out while in my highchair. I pointed to my mouth with my forefinger and gurgled, "ea, ea." Translation: "Eat! Eat! And so, the die was cast.

When I was seven, I asked a rotund visiting relative how she had ever gotten so fat. She blithely answered, "It's a long story." My older sister, you know, the purloiner of my capital gains and sugary confections, ran to my mother immediately and told her what I'd done. Getting me in trouble was my sister's favorite pastime. Mom came after me with fire in her eyes and I knew at that moment my life was over. She wanted to make sure I'd never do such rude a thing again, and so spanked me soundly with a shoe. The punishment did the trick. I never did ask that question of anyone again. But now, I'm the one answering, "It's a long story." What goes around comes around, I suppose. Anyway, I'm Santa Claus; I'm supposed to be fat.

Over the years, many well meaning friends have said, "You're not fat; you're just a big guy." It's true, I am a big guy. I'm also a fat guy. I'm a big fat guy. Overweight has been a life-long battle for me. I have always been somewhat heavy. I have been called everything from Shamu to Fat Boy. No one would ever accuse me of suffering from anorexia. I am however plagued with a severe case of bulimia. The problem is I always forget to induce vomiting after I eat.

The way I look at it is if one is obese, he can sit around feeling sorry for himself or do something about it. I chose the latter. I became Santa Claus. Whenever I put on the suit, the

Dear Santa,
How are the reindeer doing exspesly Roudlph. What kind of cookies do you whant, Oreos, Chocolate Chip. or Sniker dodles? Do the Reindeer Like the Carots I give them?
~~Love~~ from Nina

Dear Santa,
How are you? How is Roudolph and the other reindeer? How is Mrs. Claus? Have I been good this year? Do you want the same cookies as last year? I really, really want those decks of pokemon cards that I have wanting.

Have a merry Chistmas!

Leah

answer to the question, "Does this make me look fat?" is; "I certainly hope so." Nevertheless, like many pleasingly plump folks every January second, my inner thin child takes over, and I am at the gym huffing and puffing atop the treadmill determined that this is the year I will get my weight under control. (Invariably I'm always next to some Lycra-clad twenty-five pound woman who is complaining about gaining half a pound over the holidays. I have a terrible urge at that point to tackle the wench and force-feed her, a cheesecake.) By January fifteenth, my resolve to get trim and fit begins to wane. My inner fat child then takes the helm and says, "Have another Krispy Kreme, Santa!"

Throughout my life, I have also been on most every stupid diet known to man. I'm quite sure the majority of diet plans are developed by people with a sadistic sense of humor. I mean have you ever tasted most diet bars? If you like the flavor of industrial waste coupled with saw dust they're marvelous. I just happen to find Godiva chocolate somewhat more marvelous. Sorry, but Santa and diet bars just don't mesh.

There are many cases where one can eat himself out of a job, but Santa is one you can eat yourself into. Health issues aside, being hefty works well for playing Santa. Could you really trust a svelte Kris Kringle? Case in point, several years back I was crossing the street after auditioning for an opera company in downtown Los Angeles, when I spotted a man dressed as Santa Claus ringing a bell. As I got closer, I realized he wasn't with the Salvation Army. The suit, literally hanging on him, was filthy and he was smoking a cigarette. I said, "You have got to be the skinniest Santa I have ever seen!" He replied, "It must be the crack, man." Needless to say, the only donation he got from me was an arched eyebrow and a shake of the head.

People are never shy when it comes to commenting or giving me advice about my ample physique. I was once asked to don my North Pole garb and pass out candy canes at a Christmas dinner party. There was very little room between the tables. I was moving a woman slightly to get by her chair when she asked, "Is that all you under there or are you wearing padding?" "It's all me," I wistfully answered. In her very broad Brooklynese, she exclaimed, "Oh my god. You're going to die!" My inclination to stomp on her was trumped by the possibility that I might not then get paid.

Children are inevitably blunt about my weight. Generally I just let their comments roll off, but I did have to stifle my laughter when six-year-old Amanda crawled up next to me as I sat in an antique sleigh and pleaded, "I'm worried about your cholesterol. I think you need to lose a little weight." I agreed with her by saying, "You're right I probably should eat carrot sticks and fruit instead of milk and cookies." Her rejoinder to that was, "Well, one or two cookies are okay, and milk is good. Just don't eat all the cookies."

I think it was a cruel joke for God not to have given me a metabolism that actually works. I guess He feels a fat Santa is best.

TO SANTA
FROM AMBER

I'LL BE GOOD.

Chapter 7

Just a Little Off the Top

(OR GET OVER THE 60'S PAL!)

Some years back, fed up with wearing synthetic hair to play Santa, I decided that Sampson had the right idea and I began to let my own hair grow. Despite many would be Delilahs with their shears at the ready and the scorn of most corporate types with an invitation for me to get over the 60's, my hair, which is now well past my shoulders, has survived unscathed. (Excepting occasional maintenance of split ends, visits to the barber chair are a thing of the past.)

As a child, my hair was always a source of consternation to me. It was wavy—all the cool kids had straight hair—and, it was a bright copper red, which I hated. It was the real bane of my existence, other than my pilfering sister, when I was growing up. I was sure that red hair coupled with freckles made me a class "A" geek. Howdy Doody, that freckle-faced, red headed cowboy puppet, had nothing on me. I was constantly harangued by neighborhood harpies chanting, "I'd rather be dead than red in the head!"

Acceptance of my look was a long time coming and I owe it to the person dubbed, "America's favorite red-head", Lucille Ball. Several years ago, I was part of a celebrity charity show that included her. In the course of a conversation, I said, "Well you know, Lucy, we red heads have to stick together." Her reply, laced with envy, was, "Yeah, honey, but you're a real red head. Mine comes out of a bottle." With Lucy's seal of approval, I was finally proud to be a red head.

When the Father Christmas phase of my life began, having red hair was once more a pain in the backside. Since, it seems absolutely essential for Santa Claus to have a white mane; I have to spray my long flowing red locks with white pigment. My wife and I were once hired to appear as Mr. and Mrs. Santa at Lionel Richie's Christmas Eve party at his home in Beverly Hills. When we arrived, his son, age 3 or 4, ran up and threw his arms around me and exclaimed, "I know you're the real Santa, you have white hair!" Remembering my talk with Lucy, I wanted to say "Yeah, kid. Thanks to a can of white hair spray." Christine Devine, a Los Angeles news anchor, hosts a feature called, "Wednesday's Child." In this she attempts to find homes for older orphan or foster children. I got to do a Christmas segment with three siblings; Jose, Monica, and Martin. They were great kids and I sure hope they were able to place them in a good home. I was particularly fond of Jose as he informed Christine I was real because of my hair. Jose's comment made me feel like all the effort I put into my hair preparation to play Santa is certainly worth it.

Of course not every child is impressed with my hair. After the color spray process, my hair has a sort of Brill-o pad texture. Once, after touching my North Pole coiffure, a precocious four year-old sitting next to me proclaimed it, "yucky fur". The hair texture, coupled with the fact that my teeth aren't exactly pearly white, was her criterion for pronouncing me a fake Santa. I reciprocated by saying "You know what sweetheart? I may not be the real Santa, but you are a real little brat!" I then picked her up, set her out of the sleigh and told her to get lost. As she wandered off, she continued yelling out, "Fake!" and I retorted with, "Brat!" And so it went on for the next couple of minutes.

Meanwhile, my photographer, having an attack of apoplexy chimed in, "Santa Joe, you can't talk to the kids that way!" Okay, so I'm not proud of it. I am not sure what being locked in a battle of wits with a four-year-old says about my level of maturity. I guess I was just having a bad Santa hair day.

Dear Santa,?
how are you?
I hope Roudolph Doing
well too and Mrs. cloze.
have I been good? will I
git a present? I Love
you santa and Mrs cloze.
I wish I was There.
I hope your elves are
doing good

Love,
Kevin

Chapter 8

"He That Hath a Beard"

(OR THE AMALGAMATED ORDER OF REAL-BEARDED SANTAS)

Santa Claus is probably best identified by his most prominent facial feature—his beard. William Shakespeare said, "He that hath a beard is more than a youth, and he that hath no beard is less than a man."

I first grew my beard out when I was twenty-seven. It was dark red with two large and very pronounced streaks of white. Coincidentally, it was at this point everyone began telling me I would make a great Santa Claus. My intention was not to look like Kris Kringle, but rather Richard Chamberlain who had just starred in the mini-series, "Shogun". But destiny beckoned…

In my first flirtations with the "jolly old" role, I employed a beard made of synthetic hair which tied around the ears. I did that because I wanted to hide my own dark-red beard. Doubtless, you can imagine how ridiculous I looked with my own beard peeking out from behind a face full of fake hair. You would think I should have been smart enough to realize there were products to whiten my beard—but alas, no! After several less-than-stellar commercial auditions as St. Nick, where the fake beard just hung and refused to move with my mouth, I finally figured that one out! In a very few years, my beard turned completely white on its own.

Shortly after my decision to wear only my real hair and beard, I was cast in a Santa commercial for a German catalog company. The shoot was on the back lot of Universal Studios. There were nine other Santas in the commercial as well. I bonded with all of them. I loved listening to their stories. Being the youngest Santa, I had very few of my own. There was a great spirit of camaraderie between us. One or two of the guys put their heads together and formed an Elks Lodge-like fraternity out of our group. We are called the Amalgamated Order of Real-Bearded Santas. The group has now grown to national prominence with several hundred members. We get together for an annual banquet to catch up, share anecdotes and job opportunities. My membership in this group has done more good for my career than any of the acting unions to which I belong.

Having a real beard lends credibility to my Santa persona. Whenever children ask me if I'm the real Santa, I invite them to tug on my beard. That is sufficient for most kids, as they reason a real beard equals a real Santa. It doesn't always work. One precocious six-year-old came into the Santa house, and pronounced me a fraud because I wasn't at the North Pole. In reply, I told her to tug on my beard. She declined insisting, "Your beard may be real, but you're still not the real Santa." Not wanting to leave it at that, I said, "I don't believe you're a real little girl."

"Yes I am!"

"No you're not. You're a little person in little girl's clothes."

She then plucked a hair out of her head and thrust it into my face. "See, I am a little girl, my hair is real!"

I replied, "Your hair may be real, but you're not."

She turned from me in frustration and pouted, "O just forget it." I was feeling a little guilty because, in reality, radical skin cancer surgery on my face has made it impossible for me to grow a complete mustache. So my claim to be a real-bearded Santa has been slightly compromised for the past couple of years.

I purchased an expensive human-hair replacement I felt blended in quite well with my beard. One smart aleck pre-teen realized (upon close examination) that my mustache wasn't real, and proceeded to rip it off my face in the interest of showing off for his brothers. Needless to say, this young upstart found that messing with this Santa's facial hair earned him a large black mark in North Pole reckoning, and coal in his stocking for many Christmases to come. I don't think he'll be pulling a stunt like that again for a very long time.

And so, "He that hath a beard may be a Santa, but he that hath no mustache goeth to Beverly Hills and hath one grafted in!" And so I did.

Dear santa
how are you and
the elves and Mrs.
Claws. Can you
a A maikirкca girl doll bring me

PS. Bing my brother
cloal

Emily

Dear Santa,

I was wondering, can you bring me a kitten? Not for me, but for my cat. I can't explain how my other kitten died. I also want a... pobo stick, a drum, and a 10 foot robot with a nuculr missle, food and drink storage and a fort bidder.

P.S. I've been extemle Good, kind of.

Love John

Chapter 9

Almost Human

(OR SKIP TO MY LOO)

One of my favorite places to appear as Santa is at The Grove, a wonderful shopping center between Hollywood and Beverly Hills. The Santa House they have created there is fabulous. The Grove is very close to CBS Studios where I appeared as Santa on the Wayne Brady show. At the end of the taping I had to rush immediately back to The Grove to tape a segment of Christine Devine's adoption feature, "Wednesday's Child". As a consequence of the lights, my having to rush, the warm weather, and being clothed in crushed velvet. I was a mass of sweat by the time I returned. Since Santa Claus is a mythical figure, it's always a bit of a shock for kids to find out he's actually human. One potential adoptee, Jose (whom I mentioned previously), was taken aback when he exclaimed,

"You're sweating!"

I said, "Sure. It's hot."

"So, you really sweat?"

"Yes, I'm a human being."

"Do you wash your clothes?"

"Of course!"

"Do you have to take baths?"

"Every day."

"Really?"

"Yeah."

"Wow!"

Like all humans, Santa also has to occasionally make use of the water closet to address biological functions. Four year-old Ryan found this out first hand. He was alone in his grandmother's master suite watching cartoons. I came bounding in dressed in my Santa suit prior to my appearance before his grandmother's philanthropic group assembled in the living room. I greeted him and quickly skipped to the loo (bathroom). Apparently, having Santa Claus appear in person in the middle of the day to use the bathroom was a bit too much for Ryan. He felt his only option to deal with the situation was to hide behind the curtains. When his Aunt Amy came in to check on him she inquired why he was hiding. Quite shaken, he croaked, "Aunt Mamie, Santa Closet is in the baffroom!"

On another occasion, at the end of my Santa stint, I availed myself of the facilities before going on to the next stop. While washing my hands I heard several comments:

"Santa's in the bathroom."

"Is not! Santa doesn't have to go to the bathroom."

"Yes he does. I saw him go in."

"Hey you guys. Santa Claus is in the bathroom."

I stupidly thought if I delayed my departure from the water closet for a couple of minutes, the excitement over my being in there would die down. No such luck. I exited to a crowd of some ten or twelve youngsters all looking at me in disappointed wonder. I swore under my breath and exclaimed, "Well, kiddies, you've just witnessed a miracle." I would be interested to find out if that experience will drive any of them into analysis when they're older.

Seeing Santa eating is another human activity that is hard for some people to swallow. (Pun intended.) A couple of years back, though the doors to the Santa House were shut and there was a sign saying Santa was temporarily out, a mother entered with her child in tow. I was in the process of eating a quick lunch. She pointedly said, "Look, honey, Santa's eating a sandwich."

I responded with the first thing that came to mind, and plaintively said "I try to eat more healthy things, but they keep forcing me to eat carbohydrates. Apparently Santa has to have a big belly." Turning to leave, the mother explained to her child, "Let's leave Santa to his lunch. We don't want him wasting away to nothing!"

When children catch me in situations where the illusion of Santa Claus might be spoiled, I feel a bit guilty. But sometimes stuff just happens. After all Santa is only human.

Dear Santa,

I would like a Power puff girl tent. And a Diva doll. And a giant doll house. And a Olsen Twin dolls. And a barbie van. And a singing Machine, And a stuffed animala dog. And a game boy color, And Barbie doll has extra long hair. And a power puff girl sleeping bag. And a Kelly doo. I'v been a really good firl this year and I try helping my brother. And I am teaching him how to be a good boy. I love you santa. I will give you milke and cookies.

love Carrie

Dear Santa

I wood like a rasor x strem and a joll girl barby a firby and dancingDebe barbie mermaid bobbil extreeme animal alleyblack dog barbietons pawer welle barby tons barbieairplane sea rae remoye contror am fm stereocdplayerand britneyspears oop's idiliagainscd teckno meandmy shadow finger nail fancies angelica fashion factor Britney spears doll oops idid it again Barbie bech house a reyle hamtsr a gamboy in sinck cd

Love Rebecca

Chapter 10

Keep Your Shirt On Pal

(OR DUDE, I THINK YOU JUST HAD A WARDROBE MALFUNCTION)

"Wardrobe malfunction" has become a catch-phrase in our pop culture. It is nothing new to me. I have had a whole history of them in the course of my performing career as well as my everyday life.

One of my major wardrobe snafus took place at a large coastal mall in southern California. The dry cleaners there nearly ruined my new and only Santa suit. In the several days it took them to repair their mistake, I was forced to wear an ill-fitting rental. At the end of one of our work days (while wearing that accursed replacement) I needed some cash. I made my way to the ATM located right in the middle of the mall. As I stood there ready to procure my cash, I felt a sudden draft. A second later I heard a fellow say, "Damn, Santa, you just lost your pants!" To my chagrin, I discovered it was true. A couple of women were scandalized as they witnessed the situation. I nonchalantly folded the cash into my wallet, pulled up my Santa trousers, and said to the onlookers, "You don't see that everyday do you, sweetheart?" I then tossed my head back and made a grand exit, befitting royalty.

At the end of each Christmas season, I return to my professional acting career. I mentioned previously having been in a production of "Annie Get Your Gun". It was there I experienced one of my most embarrassing costume dramas. Because I am much larger than the average "Joe", obtaining wardrobe for me is frequently challenging. The costumers had a problem finding pants large enough for me when I played Buffalo Bill.

Blissfully unaware that my costume had malfunctioned during one performance, I was beginning to believe I was a comic genius. Every time I turned to the audience for a line delivery, they erupted into a sea of laughter. I remember reasoning, "If I'm this funny, I'd better look into doing stand-up comedy." At the end of the scene, I was still basking in the glow of my comedic prowess when a dancer ran past and chortled, "Did you see that? Joe's zipper broke on stage!" It was then the stark realization hit me that I was not going to be the next great comedian, and that I had just spent the last ten minutes flashing 3,500 audience members. I didn't even look down to see if it was true. I just trudged back to wardrobe and handed them my pants.

There are times, however, when wardrobe shouldn't be tampered with. Let me explain. Between Santa gigs, I sometimes work in the office at a local theater. On one of these occasions, my desk was placed so that my back was to the door. I was waiting for the son of a well-known crooner to arrive so I could help him with a special project. He was hours late. Tired of waiting, I decided to amuse myself and the secretary by rifling through the lost and found drawer. Like most actors, I too am unable to resist costumes and props. Amongst the treasures in the drawer, I found a woman's scarf, a pair of sunglasses, and an umbrella. I tied the scarf around my head, put on the sunglasses and began twirling the umbrella. In a high falsetto, I recited, "Awake me early, Mother, for I am to be Queen of the May!" Just then, I heard a distinctly deep male voice behind me say, "I'm looking for Joe." I whipped around and froze like a reindeer caught in the headlights. It would have been a nice moment for a catastrophic earthquake or other natural disaster. If Junior Crooner has a sense of humor, it certainly wasn't in evidence that day.

Even so, there has to be time for fun in everyone's life. Santa Claus likes to have a good time as well. One summer, one of my upper management elves, Dave, and I decided to go to Lake Powell for a short vacation. This was a highly unusual vacation for me because as a mercy to mankind I rarely let myself be seen in public wearing shorts or a swimsuit. At any rate, Dave was determined to teach me to water ski. I had my doubts, but agreed to try. The wardrobe malfunction I experienced there had nothing to do with a special appearance though I did have an audience.

Anyway, one afternoon, I got into the skis hoping at some point to find myself flying gracefully over the water. Unfortunately, the boat simply wasn't powerful enough to make that happen. After dozens of unsuccessful attempts we gave up. So Dave tossed me a "boogie board" hoping I could at least have some fun in the water. Sadly, when Dave hit the gas, the force of the water savagely tore my swim trunks off. I found myself giving everyone on Lake Powell a whale of a good show. As my dignity sunk slowly in the west with my swim trunks, it hit me that I had just experienced a "lack of wardrobe" malfunction.

Clothes make the man. Costumes make the actor. The Red Suit makes the Santa. Wardrobe malfunctions can truly make them the butt of a joke.

DEAR
    SANTA,

MY NAME IS JUSTIN.
I'VE BEEN A GOOD BOY ALL
YEAR.
FOR CHRISTMAS
    I'D LIKE A HUGE PRESENT.

THANKS YOU

LOVE
    JUSTIN.

Dear, Santa

How are the raindeer doing
and do the ELFS ever get
In truble? How fast do
your raindeer go? How do
you take off? is thair a door
how big is the door. Let
me gess 30ft, probly.

Love, Andrew

Chapter 11

Dash Away, Dash Away, Dash Away All

(OR IF YOU'RE THE REAL SANTA, WHERE'S YOUR REINDEER?)

Perhaps Santa's most important accoutrement is his mode of transportation. As you have probably surmised from previous chapters, I am in no way a petite personage. Ergo, the miniature sleigh mentioned in "The Night Before Christmas" is little better than a joke in my case. I would never be able to fit in it, or get it off the ground. And, the eight tiny reindeer would die in the attempt. A more realistic vehicle would be a huge sleigh like Buddy's in the movie, "Elf".

The bulk of my Santa Claus appearances a few seasons back, took place at an outdoor shopping venue which provided a beautifully restored antique sleigh as their Santa photo site. For the record, I did look rather fabulous in it. Though the sleigh was full-sized, there still wasn't enough room for me to sit comfortably. I was really crammed in. Naturally most everyone who came for a picture wanted to squeeze in next to me. It was perhaps the first time in my life where I began to have feelings of empathy for sardines.

I was particularly uncomfortable one warm afternoon when the photographer managed to pack an entire family into the sleigh and then sat their four-year-old son on my knee. But the topper was when the little imp turned with a mischievous twinkle in his eye and pronounced, "I'm going to fart on you." Sandwiched in as I was, there was no escape. I just smiled and replied flatly, "Great." I really wanted to say, "Watch it, kid, or I'll have the reindeer use you for a trampoline."

Speaking of reindeer, I can't tell you how weary I got that season of being asked, "Hey, Santa, where's your reindeer?" Well, the question did actually beg to be asked. Saint Nick's sleigh without reindeer does present a bit of an incomplete picture. I really had to dip into the barrel of my creativity to come up with answers that would satisfy the inquisitive little ones. Some bought the line I strung them, others didn't— them I always tried to buy off with candy canes. The reindeer question even popped up in an on-camera interview that year with a local weatherman. I told him the reindeer were "union" and I had to give them a certain amount of time off before the big day. (I also expressed my concern over the elves embracing collective bargaining as well. What's a Jolly Old Elf to do?)

When I wasn't available to play Santa on any given day that year, my friend, Mario, was my replacement. When asked the whereabouts of the sleigh pullers, he answered that they were out back being fed and watered. Not satisfied with that reply, a three-year old lad began to sniff the air suspiciously, and blurted, "I don't smell any reindeer s—t!" Some kids are just too smart for their own good.

Recently, after appearing as the North Pole Duo at a residential Christmas party, Mrs. Claus and I tried to make a fast track back to our vehicle. On the verge of a clean get-away, we were caught by one of the children who was too quick for us. He was horrified when he saw us getting into our car. "Hey wait a minute," he bellowed, "You're a fake! You're not the real Santa. The real Santa has reindeer and a sleigh. You drive a Navigator, and I'll bet it doesn't even fly!" My wife gently patted him on the arm and responded, "Oh, honey, you've never seen Santa drive!"

Where are those wretched reindeer when you need them?

Dear Santa

I hope that you are

doing good with
all the randere
and misses clos
Say Helloe to
the randere and
mises clos for me.
Loves
Jenna

Chapter 12

One Lump of Coal,

(OR TWO?)

I am not sure what it is about a visit to Santa Claus that strikes fear into the heart of so many children. Perhaps it's a reaction to the overwhelming costume. I do understand that fear. I had a similar reaction when I was in Kindergarten. One day, a guy came to our class dressed as a clown. He had on huge rubber shoes, giant rubber ears, and a big polka dot jumper. He looked at me and asked if I would like to accompany him to Africa to hunt for gum drops. I was perfectly horrified and declined straightaway. Yeah, like I was going to follow some clown in a costume with big rubber ears to another continent to look for candy, I don't think so! Other children, whose sugar addiction was stronger and whose parents hadn't done the "stranger-danger" lesson, were eager to volunteer for the venture.

There are times when I prefer children to have a little trepidation when they encounter a person in costume. Then they stay on their toes and are more apt to be respectful. My feeling comes with a cause. One Halloween I represented my friend's costume shop dressed as the "California Raisin"—an endearing advertising icon. I was to greet a group a first-graders at a YMCA pumpkin patch. Little did I know I was walking straight into "Children of the Corn". When I showed up, the kids made an immediate beeline for me. They began moving menacingly around me in a circle like a cat toying with his food before the kill. The little dears saw the "Raisin" as a big, dumb, punching bag. While I was being bludgeoned with hitting, spitting and kicking, their teacher just stood there and watched as if her morning coffee had been laced with Prozac. I practically had to enlist the National Guard to escape alive. So, you can see why I prefer the children to be timid and respectful when they approach the costume I wear.

On the other hand, though I like children to be respectful when they see Santa, I want them to feel I'm approachable. I certainly don't want them to be fearful. Most of the children and parents I see are pretty cool and a pleasure to be around. I am never put off or offended by children whose fear of Santa or his costume results in a spate of tears. But I do find it difficult when the tantrum is not genuine fear—just the little tyke's control drama. This is the child who repeatedly proves to his parents that they are not really in charge. He knows screaming, throwing a fit, and generally making a scene will make Mommy and Daddy fold like a cheap pup tent. There are no two ways about it—this child is a brat. Webster's defines "brat" as a spoiled or unruly child. "Mama's little angel", "daddy's little bundle of joy", and "precious" mean the same in my book. And, as Santa Claus, I've met my share of children to whom I would cheerfully give a lump of coal.

There is actually nothing wrong with these children—they are just kids, not adults. Their behavior is sometimes created by the misguided idea that indulgence is the same as love. Decrying indulgence, humorist Erma Bombeck once told me the secret to rearing children successfully was to let them take their own falls. In other words, loving a child also means teaching him manners, discipline, and personal responsibility.

As Santa Claus, I have a unique opportunity to assist the parent in reinforcing that view. When all else fails, maybe the visit to Santa's house should be put off for a while and the child should be taken somewhere and soothed. If the adult care-giver chooses to ignore the overwrought child's state of mind and brings them in anyway, they should remember that this Jolly Old Elf has ready access to a lump of coal.

Dear Santa,
How do you go to evey house in the wold. and still make it in time for diner? Wy do you have so miny elvs? Hwo makes you diner? Wy do you have a nody list and a good list? You are the coolest man in the wold.

love,
Ian

Chapter 13

Out of the Mouths of Babes

(OR THE IRREFUTABLE WISDOM OF YOUTH)

The best part about playing Santa is hearing what the children have to say. Their wisdom and reasoning is absolutely profound at times, and sometimes it is just downright hilarious.

Here's one that left me chortling for days. Each year the tree-lighting ceremony at The Grove brings in tens of thousands of people. You can imagine the lines this creates for visits to Santa. My wife was sitting outside the entrance to the Santa House. A young lad of about four was trying with all his might to see in the window. He was a little too short, so he was yelling exasperatedly at his father, "He's in there isn't he, Dad?"

His father, peering in the window replied, "Yes son, he's in there all right."

The boy groaned dejectedly and sighed, "Mom won't let me see him tonight, will she?"

"Son, the lines are really long, and she's just being Mom."

Ramming his balled hands on his hips, he retorted, "Yeah, a bitch!"

My wife nearly fell off her bench in surprise as the embarrassed parent hurriedly ushered his son away from shocked faces.

A different lad surprised me by pointedly stating his desire for distinctly *un-boy-like* Christmas gifts during his visit with me. He said, "I want all girly stuff—Barbie, Easy-Bake ovens, Hello Kitty, and make-up. Stuff like that."

I answered with a raised eyebrow and a hesitant "Okay."

In explanation, he replied, "You see, I really, really like girls. And I figure that if I have all girly stuff, the girls will want to come and play with me." There was no way to refute that logic.

Another child who knew exactly what she wanted was Madeline. One afternoon this charming three-year-old ran and jumped into my lap. After she made herself comfortable, I asked her what she'd like for Christmas. She thought for a moment and said, "I don't need anything."

I was stunned and asked, "Are you sure there is nothing

you want?"

"Well, there is one thing."

"What's that?"

"I want my brother to be here so I can play with him."

I began to worry that there had been a death or a divorce, and gently inquired, "Well, sweetheart, where is your brother?"

Pointing to her mother, who was nine months pregnant, she chirped merrily, "He's in there. And I want him to come out for Christmas so I can play with him." I make it my policy to never argue with kids who know exactly what they want.

On another occasion, after finishing a Mr. and Mrs. Santa appearance at Bloomingdale's, we were tracked down by six-year-old Mary. "Santa! Santa!" A big hug followed as Mary introduced herself. I asked the inevitable question to which she responded, "I wish for God to give me a good life." The wisdom of Solomon in such a small package. Why wasn't I that smart when I was six?

It has been said that every adult needs a child to teach, it's the way adults learn. At least it's the way this Santa gains wisdom.

Children are constantly barraged with media messages informing them they can't possibly be happy without the biggest, the brightest, and the most expensive new toy. Since that message is so ingrained, a child who can set it aside is unusual.

One Saturday evening as we were about to close up shop, three-year-old Ashley hurriedly approached Santa's sleigh ahead of her mother. Ashley let me know straight away that she hadn't come to ask for a present, but to give me one instead. She handed me an obviously child-wrapped package. Her mother said, "This was all her idea. She was afraid Santa might not get any presents, and she wanted to make sure he would get at least one." Upon opening the present, I found a well-worn cloth bunny rabbit. "This is her favorite stuffed animal," he mother informed me. I was in shock.

When I recovered, I gave Ashley a warm hug and a kiss on the cheek. Happy at my response, she began to amuse herself by looking around the sleigh. This gave me the chance to surreptitiously return the bunny to her mother. I requested that she tell Ashley the elves had made an exact copy so we could both have one. And now, whenever I see a stuffed rabbit, I think of Ashley. Ashley, at age three, was already a remarkable human being.

Britney and her grandmother came in the Grove Santa house for a visit one day. They were both warm and charming. I noticed Britney looking around, but I didn't pay much attention, since lots of children like to scope it out. I did notice Britney whisper something into her grandmother's ear, after which they quickly exited. A short time later, the duo reappeared and handed me a box from Tiffany & Company. I found a beautiful sterling silver bell inside. I stuttered an overwhelmed "Thank You."

Britney gave me a kiss on the cheek, saying "Here's your bell, Santa." Then she skipped out, giggling as she went. Following Britney, her grandmother turned and winked a "Merry Christmas."

Several times, there have been children who come to me with a handful of coins. I tell them, "What would make me really happy is for you to give this gift to a charity that will care for less-fortunate children." They are always happy to comply.

Spencer Breslin, child star of "The Kid", happened by Santa's house one evening. In response to my standard inquiry, he said, "I'm good. I just wish for all the poor children in the world to have food and clothes and a Merry Christmas."

I wish more adults were like these kids. It all leaves me shaking my head and wondering, "Who's the Santa here anyway?"

Dear King Santa,

I'm Sorry to WRIte you on short notice I'm a terminally ill childs ~~SUFFERING~~ Suffering from Violent Body Spasams My Mommy likes to call them the Shakes. The Doctors says that ~~xhsjkkpw~~ These spasams well get worster and BadдеR and will eventually snap my spinal cord and I will die

I don't want no toys for X MASS I just want you to make me Better Thank you VERY Much King Santa

I love you
Chip

Chapter 14

Knock, Knock, Knockin' on St. Nick's Door

(OR YES, VIRGINIA, THERE IS A SANTA CLAUS)

I never thought playing Santa Claus would become my career, but here I am. I once had an acting coach who talked about the roles one was destined to play from out of the womb. Santa is definitely that role for me. In the beginning it was only about reluctantly donning a red suit and a pair of boots, then forcing a smile. I now whole-heartedly embrace it. As I evolved in the role, I have actually become emotionally vested in the character. It's great to be able to put on a red velvet suit, and voila, become a superhero, a persona that people love; that makes virtually everyone smile.

But, how can that be from such a rocky beginning? It's simple really. The unconditional love and trust small children have for Santa is irresistible. Three-year-old Megan decided she loved Santa so much, she declared, "When I grow up, I want to marry him. That way, I would get presents every day." I predict that whoever marries Megan will never be bored.

Child-like love notwithstanding, I at first, forcefully resisted my fate, making the transformation into Mr. Claus long and agonizing. It began with my complete loathing for the idea. Along the way there were embarrassments and anger. But there were also a whole lot of laughs as I finally completed the transformation. The constant through it all has been the children. They eventually won me over. When I was most resistant to the metamorphosis, children, with their wonderment and complete lack of guile, had me saying, "Well…maybe." And later, "You know, being Santa is kind of fun." I found repeatedly connecting with children emotionally was pure magic.

My Beauty-and-the-Beast-like transformation has spilled over into other areas of my life as well. Most of our friends and neighbors introduce me and my wife as Mr. and Mrs. Claus. On our last vacation, we were invited as special guests to a rehearsal of the Mormon Tabernacle Choir. Upon introducing us to the choir, director, Craig Jessop, made a point of telling everyone that we were actually Mr. and Mrs. Santa. This was particularly apropos since the rehearsal was for a Christmas album. The choir and orchestra members were thrilled that the Santa Claus's came all the way from the North Pole just to inspire their rehearsal. (I am not sure whether our presence in the Tabernacle will make the album better, but you never know.) Being a part of that choir practice put me in the mood to start the holiday season right then. A little Christmas all year round would make the world a better place, I think.

Being the Claus's has even affected the way we shop. Recently, when we purchased a new vehicle, our major concern was that Santa would look good in it. Becoming Santa Claus has literally changed my entire life.

Now, I anticipate each new holiday season. More than that, I really look forward to the parents and children I will meet knowing they will help me refine the role.

We have all been affected by the cynicism of a cynical age. I too was caught up in that cynicism. Francis P. Church said it best in his famous editorial "Yes, Virginia, There is a Santa Claus". "No Santa Claus? Thank God he lives and lives forever. A thousand years from now, Virginia, nay 10 times 10,000 years from now, he will continue to make glad the heart of childhood."

So, I have finally arrived at my destiny. I knocked at the door of the North Pole, walked in and found myself. I can now assure you that Santa Claus is real. I know it for a fact.

And so, with a dash away, dash away, and a Ho! Ho! Ho!
Merry Christmas to all, and to all a goodnight.

— Santa J.O.E.